Real Estate Success

You Can Succeed at Real Estate

Jeff Davis
Real Estate Investor

Greetings

My name is Jeff Davis. The book you are beginning to read is entitled "Real Estate Success." It is my hope and desire that you will find principles and concepts that will help you to achieve the levels of success you desire to achieve in Real Estate.

I am no novice to this game. I have had my Real Estate license active in two states. I began as a part time Real Estate Salesperson working in a Century 21 office while I worked full time as a loan officer. This experience taught me mortgage financing.

When I made the decision to get into this full time I got my Brokers license and was made Managing Broker at the office with 35 agents who reported to me. I wanted to invest myself so in time I began purchasing small properties and acting as a landlord. This was a great learning experience for me.

In my career I have been a Realtor with my own Real Estate company, a landlord and I have managed a Real Estate Investment company with 195 single family homes and a 64 unit apartment building. I have worked on homes and sold them at a profit.

This book is a compilation of various topics pertaining to real estate. I am not trying to provide you with an exhaustive study on the subject. There are many good books available out there. This is my effort to help others benefit from the knowledge I have gained in over 20 years of dealing with properties.

I suggest you read each chapter one at a time, take from it what you can use and add to your learning knowledge.

Happy Investing,

Jeff Davis

The Best Job You Could Ask For

Once you are grown and on your own, undoubtedly you will need a job. The question is not whether or not you will find a job (given the state of our current economy it can be a challenge) but whether or not you will find the job you were created to do.

We spend on average 40 hours a week working. Take the time to get to ready for work, the time to travel to and from our jobs and you could easily spend 50 plus hours a week just doing work related events. There are 168 hours in a week so about 1/3 of our time is spent centering around this thing we call "work".

That being the case, we should try our best to have jobs that fulfill us. We need to be both challenged while performing our job and rewarded when we do a great at it. You cannot have these results if you go out and just "get a job". So many people go to work to earn a paycheck and provide for them and their families. This makes it hard to pursue the career that is meant for you if you are not fulfilled at your current position.

Am I saying quit your job? Not necessarily. What I am saying is you need to focus on what you want to do, what you love to do and what you would be willing to do even if you were not being paid. Focus the 1/3 of your life you spend working being as productive as possible while making the living you hope to have so you can enjoy life.

What is the best job you could hope for? I believe it is a job that offers you the following characteristics;

Financial Security - it is a sad thing to get up every day, spend all this time working and not earning enough to be secure. How much is that? Based on your budget you want a job that pays your bills, allows you to save a portion each paycheck and invest in your future. If I make $5000 a month and my monthly obligations are $3000 a month I have $2000 "margin" to work with each month. Margin is important in maintaining financial security.

Financial Freedom - this involves working to the point where you are not a slave to your job. It's been said that most people are only 30 days away from financial ruin. Can you take a month off, get no check from work and still live as you live with your job? If not, you are not free yet. Strive to get to the place where you have the reserves to hold you over for a while if you become unemployed.

Passive Income Sources - Let's say you have a good job and in addition you own real estate that gives you $2500 a month after the bills are paid. This is considered a passive income source. Increase these different sources for passive income and your job becomes much easier to work.

The best job to have is the one that allows you to grow into total freedom.

How to Build a Real Estate Investing Career

Real Estate Investing can be a great career choice for the person who wants to build that type of business. And it is a business. One must start off looking at it as a business and operate it daily as you would any other business.

Let me offer you a few tips on building a successful real estate investing career;

1) Decide on what you want - there are so many ways you can build your business.
A) Wholesaling - many people start off here. They find a property and then sell it to another investor and make a fee for doing the transaction.
B) Rehabbing- If you are OK with fixing and repairing houses (or overseeing a crew that does that) then this may be the way to go.
C) Land lording - here you purchase and hold real estate receiving rental payments each month
D) Selling - here all you do is sell the real estate you acquire looking to do little or no work to it. You look for either homeowners or investors.

2) Decide on how you want to get there -If you want you can do either one or all of these methods. The key is to determine how you want to spend your days dealing with real estate. For a wholesaler you will need to create a network of investors to buy your deals. For a rehabber you will need to assemble a crew of professionals, observe local building codes, etc. For the landlord you will need to find good cash flowing rentals and deal with either tenants or property management companies. To sell you will either need a real estate license or connect with local realtors to sell your deals.

3) Set financial goals for your investing career - how much money do you want to make monthly? Yearly? Wholesaling provides quick money ($2,000-$10,000 range): Rehabbing provides larger payday but takes months to realize ($15,000-$40,000 or more); Land lording provides steady monthly rental income; Selling can give you commission or owners income.

4) Think long term - whichever strategy you choose, look to develop long term systems that will sustain your business. Cash flow is king so establish ways to keep the cash flowing into your business and before long your business will be taking care of you nicely.

5) Use LLC's and Corporations- these will help protect your assets and make title transfers easier to convey to buyers.

Real Estate Investor, Part A

If you have decided to become a Real Estate Investor you have made a good choice. In order to be successful in this decision there are a few questions you need to ask yourself:

1) Do I want to be a fulltime or part-time Investor? - The fulltime Investor makes the majority of his income by his activities in real estate. They don't have another job and focus on doing real estate. The part time Investor has another fulltime job and does this on the side. You can benefit in either direction, you just have to decide which way you want to move.

2) What kind of Investor do you want to be?- There are various types of real estate (single family homes, multifamily homes of 2-4 units, apartment buildings, office buildings, land, etc.). Not every investment is ideal for every investor. You have to decide what your personal comfort level is and then pursue that focus.

When I was taking my real estate classes our teacher was a woman who owned 40 single family homes. She told us she chose homes because the tenants handled most of the maintenance and the turnover rate was low. She had developed a system for managing her homes and it worked for her.

I met another lady who was a fulltime schoolteacher and part-time investor. Her and her partner both had full time jobs and decided to buy a house, fix it up and sell it. She only sold 2 houses a year but consistently made over $30,000 a year. For her this was great.

I personally have owned single family homes, multi units and apartment buildings. I prefer apartment buildings because you have your tenants localized, you can generate impressive rents and fix apartments without having to travel to different properties. I know investors who hate apartment buildings. You have to decide what type of investor you want to be.

3) How much money do you want to make from your Real Estate Investing? - The answer to this question will help you to determine what you should invest in. Single family homes can be good rentals but if you are looking for a large cash flow you will need to rent a lot of them out. $125 per month net income from a single family home would be great. If you want more income then you may have to look at moving up to multifamily properties or apartment buildings. Office complexes can offer great income but require professional management to optimize the return on your investment.

Being a Real Estate Investor is a great career. Just decide on what type of Investor you plan on becoming. Then just do it.

Real Estate Investor Part B

We spoke on how a Real Estate Investor needs to focus on what aspect of real estate they want to be involved in. Today we will look at how important it is to create a business model for your investing so that it won't turn into another job.

In the book "Rich Dad, Poor Dad" the author talks about 4 quadrants for working; the employee, the self - employed, the business owner and the money investor. Each has a distinct characteristic that sets it apart from the others. When you decide to become a Real Estate Investor you have to decide which quadrant you want to work in.

Employees typically work set hours and can expect a set pay. Investors don't see that happening when they get into real estate. Self - Employed people are pretty much like employees except they don't have a boss. In both of these scenarios if you don't work you don't get paid.

Business owners work on their business but not in it. They have employees who do most of the work and the owners make sure the business is thriving and surviving. The money investor takes his cash and makes it work for him. He gets interest and a rate of return on his investment.

Most Real Estate Investors fall into one of the two categories; either they are self - employed or a business owner. Self- employed investors purchase properties, work on those properties, lease them, evict bad tenants, advertise vacancies, etc. It is almost like another job. For the hands on investor this is ideal. They love the feeling of being involved in the day- to-day activities going on with their properties.

The other type of investor is a business owner. He goes out and buys properties. But then he has developed a team he supervises which handles every aspect of his portfolio. Men like Donald Trump do not hang drywall or repair floors; he has employees who handle all the details for him.

Neither type of investor is wrong. You just have to decide which type of investor you want to be. If you want to be hands on and involved in the day - to- day activities of your properties, then be a self - employed investor. But if you prefer having others do that type of work so you can be free to purchase and sell your inventory, then consider running your investing like a business.

The choice is yours.

Can I Buy Real Estate With No Money Down

Can I still buy real estate with no money down? Look at the current market. There have been so many changes to how properties are financed that it would appear the no money down real estate is dead.

Yet that is not totally accurate. I think we must remember that you can buy real estate with no money down but it is very hard to buy real estate with no money. You still have other costs such as an appraisal, title insurance, property insurance and a few others.

You can still purchase property with no money down. But you have to learn how to do so in this current market. Let me share with you a few ways that have worked for me in years past.

1) I purchased a 2 flat with no money down. The seller was looking to unload a vacant building that had just been vacated by its tenants. I approached her and said I would purchase her property if I could do so with no money down. I gave her the full asking price, she paid the down payment and I got a new first loan. I did have to pay my own closing costs but I saved the money down.

Principle I learned; ask the seller for help

2) Purchased a 6 flat and got financing from a neighborhood bank. Told them I wanted a loan from them to cover the entire purchase price. Seller accepted a price that was about 90% of the appraised value of the building so I would close with automatic equity. Bank agreed to give me 100% financing if I would pledge equity I had in other property in lieu of putting down cash. I got property with 100% financing and at the closing got $5000 in credits.

Principle I learned: always ask seller for a break on the price and use equity in other investments to keep your cash

3) Purchased a LLC that own real estate. Instead of refinancing all the properties in the LLC I purchased the LLC from the owners. It was no money down to me and I paid what I owed them from the cash flow of their own investments. I will be able to sell off properties individually with proceeds going to the LLC.

Principle I learned: be creative in acquiring ownership of real estate.

You can still purchase with no money down if you are creative in your approach.

What Can A Guru Teach You About Real Estate

I have been involved in real estate for over 20 years. During that time I have been a loan officer, real estate broker, investor and managed a property management company. In addition I have spent thousands of dollars on books, resources and classes taught by the so called real estate 'gurus' of our day. I believe anyone who is serious about a career in this field does just that. But I now have insight based on my experience as a real estate professional which I want to share with you.

Gurus are those people who have been involved in real estate in some capacity and now have achieved a certain level of "success' whereby they have shifted from investing full time to teaching. They write books, conduct seminars and offer personal mentoring to students. By themselves these items are good. But let's examine what you typically pay for when you enlist the help of a guru.

1) The focus is on marketing heavily to an unsuspecting public - they buy infomercials and spend a ton on pretty packaging. They use commercials and websites to promote their supposed expertise.

2) The material offered is very basic - the information you get from these gurus is available on the internet. They seldom get into anything deep and stay on the surface with what they share. Even after spending all that money on a seminar the truth is most students make no money after completing these programs.

3) The pricing is ridiculous - when you consider hundreds of dollars for CD programs, thousands of dollars for seminars and tens of thousands for mentoring, the price points are way out of line. The only person making money is the guru. Instead of making money from real estate, they make their money from being a guru.

4) The success of the program is always dependent on the student - gurus would have you to believe that if you fail, it's your fault. That is a prevalent concept with people who focus on sharing information. But if you took a driving class and at the end couldn't drive or our children went to school and at the end couldn't read, is that only the student's fault. Guru's need to take responsibility for the information they are charging so much for.

5) Everyone acts like they have the latest "concept' in investing - there is very little new under the sun. Don't get caught up in thinking that someone has some "new" concept that will revolutionize real estate. Remember, if the

guru could make a ton of money with the concept they are teaching you, they would teach less.

Finally, many gurus end up bankrupt. Look them up after a few years and see for yourself.

The Truth About Real Estate Gurus - Part I

I have been involved in Real Estate for over 20 years. During that time I have been a Salesperson, Broker, Investor and owner of an office. At one time I have had 256 units under my management while renovating and flipping single family homes.

With this experience I thought about going into the seminar business. I could teach people how to purchase property with no money down, how to renovate and sell single family homes or how to purchase apartment buildings. I have spent thousands of dollars on many seminars in the past and felt that I could do as good a job as most of those guys.

Yet I didn't go that route. Why? Because I believe people are spending way too much money on these seminars and receiving little to no value in return.

I know that some people (like me) see all the flipping shows on TV and wonder if we can do that too. Can we make a fortune working part time? Can we quit our job in 6 months and become a full time Investor? These shows are great at creating a desire in us to do what we see being done before us.

Let me share with you some reasons you should consider before investing in these seminars;

1) The premise that you can become a successful Investor this way is false - it would be great if you could go to a seminar, spend a few thousand dollars and end up with the tools you need to launch your investing career. But the truth is dealing with real estate is very complicated. It is an area that requires specialized knowledge in order to be effective.

What is an amortization schedule? What is a hard money loan? What is L.T.V.? R.E.O.? These are some of the terms used in real estate. It can take years to get a handle on what it means to do this successfully.

2) Many gurus no longer practice purchasing, renovating, renting and selling real properties- These guys may have been active in times past but many now are not engaged in the day to day practice of doing real estate. Instead they focus on getting "students" who they promise have success.

3) The person who makes the most money is the guy giving the seminar - when you consider they charge hundreds and thousands of dollars per

person, it's not hard to do the math and see that these guys make more money teaching about real estate than investing in it.

In our next chapter we will discuss how you can invest in real estate and not pay the huge fees gurus' charge.

The Truth About Real Estate Gurus - Part II

If you watch TV you will see programs that deal with renovating real estate for sale (Flip That House, Flipping Boston, Flip or Flop, Love It or List It, Property Brothers, Flipping Vegas to name a few). I like watching these programs and watching homes that were previously wrecked turned around and made nice.

Real Estate Gurus use the success of these programs to "prey" upon an innocent public with promises of becoming rich in real estate. I find it sickening to think that many people have lost thousands of dollars on these classes and programs yet have not gotten a return on the investment.

Let me tell you some of the things I find with this type of marketing to the public;

1) You can become financially independent investing in real estate - yes, you can. Most wealthy people have real estate in their portfolio. It is a great investment vehicle and can offer many benefits to its owner.

2) Anyone can flip houses and make money - this is not true. To accurately flip a house you need to know how to purchase at the right, discounted price; you need to know how to negotiate a good deal on the renovations; you need a General Contractor who will work with you; you need a Realtor to sell your home. This is not something you can learn in 3 days and do effectively.

The reason I know this to be true (if some doubt it) is that once you ask each guru to furnish you with the % of students who make no money taking their class, the number will amaze you. There are a small number of successful students (those who at least recoup their initial investment for the class). The only person getting rich off of real estate is the guru getting rich off of the classes.

3) All you need is to pay for a class - this is a lie. If all you need is to take a class to be successful, colleges would be filled with successful students.

4) If you attend a class and don't succeed, it's the student's fault - I hate this concept most of all. To blame students because the teaching is not effective is not how good teachers teach. If your students do not achieve the results promised, the problem may be the teacher or the material.

I believe in real estate and I know you need specialized knowledge in the subject to be successful. However I don't think anyone can go to a 3 day seminar, pay thousands of dollars to a teacher and end up rich. It is not good business and not practical.

Real Estate Can (Not Will) Make You Rich

People dream about being rich all the time. There are a few ways to do that. You can inherit wealth from your family (like the Walton's or the Hilton's), you can build a successful business that brings you wealth through ownership (such as Bill Gates or Steve Jobs) or through investing (Warren Buffet or Donald Trump).

Then there is real estate. I believe that this is the best vehicle for the average person. When you want to build a nest egg that can be worth millions of dollars you can use this as the vehicle. Here are a few reasons why:

1) Appreciation - Contrary to what has happened in our economy these last few years appreciation is still one of the top reasons to own real estate. Property has a habit of increasing in value over time and you can see your investment go up in price.

2) Tax Advantages - You can use investments to lower your tax liability and create write offs for yourself. You can increase your income simply but deducting allowable rent expenses.

3) Rental Income - I like this benefit of owning property. Each month you can receive income from your investment properties that help to improve your cash flow. You can get to a point where you can live off of your rents. Some landlords do and kiss their jobs goodbye.

4) Multiple uses of equity - When you own property you can use the equity to purchase other properties or to make purchases on things you want. I remember going to buy my dream car and having the gentleman look at my income and the car I wanted. Based on my job at that moment I could not afford the car with my current payments. But when I told the salesman I also owned property and got rental income each month I walked out with my car.

5) Leverage - As you look to expand your real estate portfolio you can use one building to purchase another. I was buying a six unit building and was short on cash. I spoke with a lender and they ultimately used that equity to close on the building I wanted. Real Estate is one of the vehicles to use leverage on because people are not expected to pay cash for a property.

6) Profits from fix and flip - You can buy, fix and flip homes. If you are profitable and can save a portion of your profits, you may end up rich.

Go for it. RE Investing is a great life.

The Reality About Fix and Flip Programs

I love getting up and turning on my TV to watch the Fix and Flip programs. It is great seeing how a house which was abandoned and torn up can be transformed into a masterpiece that is a welcome change to any neighborhood. I think it is good to have someone come in and do things that improve a community.

These shows have sprung up all over, I counted at least 8 fix and flip programs in my area. I know part of the reason for that is the popularity this concept has gotten given our past real estate climate. There is a lot that we can benefit from when we watch them.

As a Real Estate Investor, I look at the programs with a slightly different focus. I wonder how accurately these shows reveal the struggles a fix and flipper has in order to be profitable. I know the shows have to be edited for TV so you can only see a portion of what goes on to make a deal work. The portions they do show focus almost exclusively on the renovations. But there is a whole lot more involved in fixing and flipping than just renovating.

I am not criticizing the shows. I want to just bring up a few items I notice when I watch them.

1) The focus on these shows is never about the money - it would seem that the shows outline looking for a property, buying it, fixing it and selling it. If the process was that simple everyone could be a flipper. But the reality is the major problem in flipping is money.

If you watch a few of the shows you will find that many of the flippers purchase these properties with cash. Yet for the average person who is looking to flip there is not $500,000 sitting in a bank account. For many of the people on TV the reason they don't talk much about money is they already have it.

If you want to enter into their world you will have to solve the money issue. You cannot flip properties broke.

2) The end profit shown when they sell is gross profit, not net profit - on average you can expect to earn $25,000-$30,000 per deal after all your expenses are paid. There are some average costs you can plug in but if you can hit the average, be grateful.

3) It's not always easy to sell the finished home - contrary to popular flip programs, unless you can offer your property at or below market, it may sit for a while. You don't want to over improve the property but you need room in the price to unload.

Watch and learn. Then read, study and go flip that house!

If You Are Rich, Why Do You Need My Money

I am a Real Estate Investor. I look for deals; put together the financing, close and either resell those properties or hold on for rental income. This is what I like doing.

It never ceases to amaze me the number of people who claim to be in a position to help you achieve your goals but can only do that if you pay them. Now I have no problem paying for services rendered. I have a problem paying when the only person who benefits is the one who receives money.

Let me explain. I am always looking for lending sources. I find some who say they can give me the money I need to purchase but I have to pay them a fee. This is to either cover insurance, to cover processing fees or administrative fees. When I was a novice in this business I use to pay these upfront fees and find lenders would never close my deals. The fees were never refunded and the only person who got paid was the lender.

I changed all that. Now I only pay for items that you have to pay upfront in order for a lender to make a decision - namely for appraisals and maybe credit reports although many run their own credit reports on you. I never pay any fees that the lender charges to process my loan. Those are administrative fees and should be paid when everyone makes money. That is at the closing.

I adhere to the principles that everyone must win. I must win. The seller must win. The lender must win. Anyone associated with a deal of mine must win. People will not work for you for long if they are constantly taking a hit and not winning in the transactions.

The same goes for all of these self-proclaimed real estate experts who have made their fortune in real estate and now look to make it big based on people paying to connect with them. You are not connecting based on "we do a deal and both get paid". No, its "you pay me a fee to help you and hopefully you will close and make some money". Problem with this philosophy is if the deal doesn't close you are not going to get your money back.

I think businesses in the 21st century have been hurt by people only trying to get money for themselves. Many of those who participated in the flip houses series on A & E have begun to have seminars. That can be good.

But to milk the public out of money promising people future riches is wrong. There is a lot more to being successful than having a system, having a mentor or spending thousands on books and CD's hoping you will emulate their success.

Rich people should not take advantage of those less fortunate and require money from them. How about using your wealth to help others do better in life.

Building Your Real Estate Portfolio

If you are serious about being in the game of real estate, then it may be time to begin to build the foundation that will grow your wealth; portfolio building.

There are a lot of ways to make money in real estate. You can buy and renovate properties for flipping. You can wholesale properties to end buyers. You can earn fees by referring properties to investors. You can get a license and sell real estate or manage other people's real estate for a fee.

But the only way to build what I call "residual income" is to build an income producing portfolio. This means that you have to develop an income stream that comes from having tenants paying rent in properties that you own.

I encourage everyone who wants to have real estate as a part of their investment portfolio to consider adding rental income properties. Even the top movie stars and athletes who develop portfolios to grow their wealth will place a portion of it in real estate. Over 90% of the people who are wealth in this country have placed a portion of their money into real estate.

Let's look at what such a portfolio can look like;

1) Single family homes - I have had as many as 195 homes under management. If you do the numbers right you can actually cash flow nicely. The challenge is making sure the income coming in does not get eaten up with mortgage payments and repairs. The good thing about having single family homes is you can pass a lot of the maintenance over to the tenant. You can also create lease to own and seller financed deals to have a steady inflow of money coming in.

2) Apartment buildings - these are my personal favorite for a number of reasons. First, you only have one location to go to for repairs, rent collections, etc. You can have an onsite maintenance man to handle minor repairs and get a few contractors to make sure you keep your building in tip top shape. When you have a vacancy in an apartment building you still have other units paying rent so your negative cash flow is not as bad as when you have a vacant single family home. It is also much harder to vandalize an apartment complex than it is a single family home.

3) Office buildings / shopping complexes - great money makers as well.

This is an entirely different animal to manage and I would suggest you get professional help unless you have experience in this one.

Buy you some real estate. Soon!

Does Real Estate Coaching Really Work?

Real Estate Coaching is big business. This is where a "guru" offers to coach you to your real estate dreams. The way it is displayed it sounds like the only people who make it in real estate are those who get coaches.

Being a sports fan and someone who played sports under coaches I will be the first to say that coaching has a ton of value. It was Michael Jordan's high school coach who gave him advice that pointed him in the path of stardom. Many legendary coaches receive accolades from their player on a regular basis and the praise is well deserved.

But when I look at a lot (not all) of the real estate gurus stressing the need for everyone to have a coach to be successful, it turns my stomach the wrong way. Sometimes I think (and this is only my opinion but it's also my article) that the focus on coaching isn't to raise up a bunch of superstar investors but to create another income stream for the coach. Consider the following;

1) Typically you have to apply to be coached (kind of like a tryout). But what they look for isn't ability or proficiency in investing. They look for people who have a heart to succeed (and who doesn't) along with the financial wherewithal to pay their fees.

2) It is not uncommon for coaching to cost anywhere from $1000 to tens of thousands of dollars. That is money that won't go into your investing program; it goes into your coach's pocket.

3) Coaches make their money on the front end. As an investor you have to make your money on the back end. Now with sports when a coach has a winning season and a team that wins often, he is rewarded with contract extensions and more money. Coaches partake in the victory of their teams. I believe real estate coaches should be rewarded when their students are hitting their goals. After all, if they are unable to hit their goals, what did they pay the coach for?

4) In real estate the chances of students even hitting mediocre results are staggering.
If you ask these coaches to tell you "how many students have you coached, how many have hit their goals and how many just paid you to say they had a coach?' Typically in the advertisements you see the successful students.

But if there are 400 students and only 40 hit their goals, 90% of them only succeeded in making their coach richer.

5) Finally, although we all need help, we really have to watch when the only way people help is to be paid. I pay my attorney to handle deals. But he knows I can hold him 100% for results. He doesn't get paid to be on my team. He gets paid to produce.

Is your coach 100% responsible for results? I would ask before parting with all my money.

Wholesaling - Does It Really Work?

There have always been seminars on how to make money in real estate. There was buy and hold, flip and now wholesaling. Seems like there is always something going on in the world of real estate.

Is this all bad, No. Buying and holding real estate for rental income and future sales is a path to great wealth. Renovating homes to "flip" (sale) later also has made a lot of investors profitable. Now the concept is wholesaling; Does it have the same guarantee of returns that buy and hold and flipping has in the past?

Let me give you a definition for wholesaling real estate. It is when you purchase a property way below value and then sell it to an Investor at a slightly higher price. The difference between what you paid for the property and what the investor pays you is your profit. That is a wholesale deal.

Does it work? Yes. But typically when you read a book on the subject or attend a seminar there are some vital components of wholesaling left out (I wonder why? Maybe it is to get you to part with your money so the seminar company can make money off of classes and not wholesaling.

I am not saying you should not engage in this activity. What I am saying is know what you are getting into before you pay lots of money to learn something you may fail at.

1) Wholesaling only works when the price is right - an ideal wholesale deal looks like this; Property is worth $100,000 when repairs are done. If repairs will cost $20,000, you need to purchase the property for no more than $45,000. $45000 and $20000 equals $65000 which is the ideal % for a wholesale deal to work. If you pay $60000 or $70000 for the property and it needs $20000 in repairs to be worth $100000, no investor will touch it. There is not enough room to generate a profit for them.

2) Wholesaling only works when a seller is highly motivated- desperate is a better word. How many sellers will release their properties to you for 65% on the value? And many times will you need it at 35%-45% of the value to make sense.

Stores may spend 30-35% on items they sell when they purchase wholesale. Even with purchasing at that rate they don't make a killing when you add in the expenses necessary to sell those items. Houses are no different.

3) In some areas of the country it is just not realistic -I reside in California where it is almost impossible to find a property with a 10% cap rate. What this means is people expect a lot of money for their properties. Getting people in California, New York and some of the other major metropolitan cities to sell to you for pennies on the dollar is unrealistic.

Be very careful before you jump into wholesaling. Save your shirt.

Fix and Flip. Fact or Fiction

There are many shows on A & E sharing the concept of fixing and flipping properties. These shows reveal how properties are purchased, rehabbed and sold. Most of the time there is a profit for the investor.

I like these shows. You get to see some great ideas on how to convert properties so they can be resold at a high price. Overall the concept is good.

The challenges I find with these programs is the information they choose to leave out. With this omission you cannot have the level of success they all seem to enjoy.

Consider;

1) The biggest challenge in fix and flipping is getting the money- this is by far the one hurdle every investor must overcome. In many of the flip shows you see investors with the cash money to purchase deals. Although this is a great place to be in, the reality is that most people don't have access to that kind of cash. So even if they were all excited about getting into fixing and flipping properties they won't see a way to get it done.

2) Lenders don't like lending to amateurs - those with money didn't get it because they are a fool. They make wise lending decisions. When you are looking to get into fixing and flipping you have to convince a lender that you know what you are doing. They all want to get their money back as soon as possible. That means you have to tell them what you think it will take to renovate the home and what it will ultimately sell for. Fortunately there are contractors and real estate agents to help you do just that.

3) Focus is more on the renovation than the resale - renovating is important. But you need to know how each renovation will impact the sales price. If it doesn't make you money in the end then you may not need to be doing it. Keeping your eye on the bottom line is key to fixing and flipping.

4) You have to buy right to sell right - there is a formula you have to follow if you want to buy right. Basically you need the purchase price and renovation costs to equal 65% of the final sales price. If you can do this there is a chance you will make money investing.

Don't buy into all the hype if you are serious about becoming an Investor. Learn what you can from the programs but do your homework before you invest and lose money.

I hope this book has provided you with some insight into the world of Real Estate.

Feel free to visit our website at www.lordshipinc.com for more info on who we are.

Visit www.amazon.com for more info on books and resources we have available.

Happy Investing!

www.ingramcontent.com/pod-product-compliance
Lightning Source LLC
Chambersburg PA
CBHW051419170526
45165CB00004BA/1887